St. Mary's High School

THE **MAKING** OF THE **MODERN WORLD**

1945 TO THE PRESENT

Culture and Customs in a Connected World

BOOKS IN THE SERIES

Culture and Customs in a Connected World

Education, Poverty, and Inequality

Food, Population, and the Environment

Governance and the Quest for Security

Health and Medicine

Migration and Refugees

Science and Technology

Trade, Economic Life, and Globalization

Women, Minorities, and Changing Social Structures

THE MAKING OF THE MODERN WORLD

1945 TO THE PRESENT

Culture and Customs in a Connected World

John Perritano

SERIES ADVISOR
Ruud van Dijk

Mason Crest

Mason Crest
450 Parkway Drive, Suite D
Broomall, PA 19008
www.masoncrest.com

Produced and developed by MTM Publishing.
www.mtmpublishing.com

President and Project Coordinator: Valerie Tomaselli
Designer: Sherry Williams, Oxygen Design Group
Copyeditor: Lee Motteler, GeoMap Corp.
Editorial Coordinator: Andrea St. Aubin
Proofreader: Peter Jaskowiak

ISBN: 978-1-4222-3635-2
Series ISBN: 978-1-4222-3634-5
Ebook ISBN: 978-1-4222-8279-3

Library of Congress Cataloging-in-Publication Data
On file

Printed and bound in the United States of America.

First printing
9 8 7 6 5 4 3 2 1

Contents

Series Introduction 6

CHAPTER 1: The "Modern" World of World War II 9

CHAPTER 2: Culture and the Cold War: 1950s and 1960s 19

CHAPTER 3: The Counterculture and East Meets West: 1960s 31

CHAPTER 4: Equal Rights and the End of the Cold War: Into the 1980s 41

CHAPTER 5: Globalization and Today's Challenges 49

Timeline 58

Further Research. 60

Index. 61

Photo Credits 63

About the Author and Advisor 64

KEY ICONS TO LOOK FOR:

Words to understand: These words with their easy-to-understand definitions will increase the reader's understanding of the text while building vocabulary skills.

Sidebars: This boxed material within the main text allows readers to build knowledge, gain insights, explore possibilities, and broaden their perspectives by weaving together additional information to provide realistic and holistic perspectives.

Educational Videos: Readers can view videos by scanning our QR codes, providing them with additional educational content to supplement the text. Examples include news coverage, moments in history, speeches, iconic sports moments and much more!

Text-dependent questions: These questions send the reader back to the text for more careful attention to the evidence presented there.

Research projects: Readers are pointed toward areas of further inquiry connected to each chapter. Suggestions are provided for projects that encourage deeper research and analysis.

Series Introduction

In 1945, at the end of World War II, the world had to start afresh in many ways. The war had affected the entire world, destroying cities, sometimes entire regions, and killing millions. At the end of the war, millions more were displaced or on the move, while hunger, disease, and poverty threatened survivors everywhere the war had been fought.

Politically, the old, European-dominated order had been discredited. Western European democracies had failed to stop Hitler, and in Asia they had been powerless against imperial Japan. The autocratic, militaristic Axis powers had been defeated. But their victory was achieved primarily through the efforts of the Soviet Union—a communist dictatorship—and the United States, which was the only democracy powerful enough to aid Great Britain and the other Allied powers in defeating the Axis onslaught. With the European colonial powers weakened, the populations of their respective empires now demanded their independence.

The war had truly been a global catastrophe. It underlined the extent to which peoples and countries around the world were interconnected and interdependent. However, the search for shared approaches to major, global challenges in the postwar world—symbolized by the founding of the United Nations—was soon overshadowed by the Cold War. The leading powers in this contest, the United States and the Soviet Union, represented mutually exclusive visions for the postwar world. The Soviet Union advocated collectivism, centrally planned economies, and a leading role for the Communist Party. The United States sought to promote liberal democracy, symbolized by free markets and open political systems. Each believed fervently in the promise and justice of its vision for the future. And neither thought it could compromise on what it considered vital interests. Both were concerned about whose influence would dominate Europe, for example, and to whom newly independent nations in the non-Western world would pledge their allegiance. As a result, the postwar world would be far from peaceful.

As the Cold War proceeded, peoples living beyond the Western world and outside the control of the Soviet Union began to find their voices. Driven by decolonization, the developing world, or so-called Third World, took on a new importance. In particular, countries in these areas were potential allies on both sides of the Cold War. As the newly independent peoples established their own identities and built viable states, they resisted the sometimes coercive pull of the Cold War superpowers, while also trying to use them for their own ends. In addition, a new Communist China, established in 1949 and the largest country in the developing world, was deeply entangled within the Cold War contest between communist and capitalist camps. Over the coming decades, however, it would come to act ever more independently from either the United States or the Soviet Union.

During the war, governments had made significant strides in developing new technologies in areas such as aviation, radar, missile technology, and, most ominous, nuclear energy. Scientific and technological breakthroughs achieved in a military context held promise for civilian applications, and thus were poised to contribute to recovery and, ultimately, prosperity. In other fields, it also seemed time for a fresh start. For example, education could be used to "re-educate" members of aggressor nations and further Cold War agendas, but education could also help more people take advantage of, and contribute to, the possibilities of the new age of science and technology.

For several decades after 1945, the Cold War competition seemed to dominate, and indeed define, the postwar world. Driven by ideology, the conflict extended into politics, economics, science and technology, and culture. Geographically, it came to affect virtually the entire world. From our twenty-first-century vantage point, however, it is clear that well before the Cold War's end in the late 1980s, the world had been moving on from the East-West conflict.

Looking back, it appears that, despite divisions—between communist and capitalist camps, or between developed and developing countries—the world after 1945 was growing more and more interconnected. After the Cold War, this increasingly came to be called "globalization." People in many different places faced shared challenges. And as time went on, an awareness of this interconnectedness grew. One response by people in and outside of governments was to seek common approaches, to think and act globally. Another was to protect national, local, or private autonomy, to keep the outside world at bay. Neither usually existed by itself; reality was generally some combination of the two.

Thematically organized, the nine volumes in this series explore how the post–World War II world gradually evolved from the fractured ruins of 1945, through the various crises of the Cold War and the decolonization process, to a world characterized by interconnectedness and interdependence. The accounts in these volumes reinforce each other, and are best studied together. Taking them as a whole will build a broad understanding of the ways in which "globalization" has become the defining feature of the world in the early twenty-first century.

However, the volumes are designed to stand on their own. Tracing the evolution of trade and the global economy, for example, the reader will learn enough about the political context to get a broader understanding of the times. Of course, studying economic developments will likely lead to curiosity about scientific and technological progress, social and cultural change, poverty and education, and more. In other words, studying one volume should lead to interest in the others. In the end, no element of our globalizing world can be fully understood in isolation.

The volumes do not have to be read in a specific order. It is best to be led by one's own interests in deciding where to start. What we recommend is a curious, critical stance throughout the study of the world's history since World War II: to keep asking questions about the causes of events, to keep looking for connections to deepen your understanding of how we have gotten to where we are today. If students achieve this goal with the help of our volumes, we—and they—will have succeeded.

—Ruud van Dijk

In Paris, U.S. servicemen and women celebrate the surrender of Japan on August 15, 1945, marking the end of World War II.

WORDS TO UNDERSTAND

annihilation: destruction.

consensus: general agreement.

fascism: ideology marked by extreme nationalist ideas, a totalitarian system of government, and a strict regimentation of public and private life.

fatalism: attitude and belief that life is subject to fate and outside of one's control.

nationalistic: devoted to one's nation.

propaganda: writings, speeches, films, and other cultural products designed to influence someone's thinking.

CHAPTER
1

The "Modern" World of World War II

We want Harry! We want Harry!" the crowd shouted. It was August 14, 1945, and President Harry S. Truman had just announced that Japan had surrendered. World War II, which began for the United States on December 7, 1941, was over. Crowds had been gathering in front of the White House all day, hoping to see the president. Finally, Truman, with his wife, Bess, at his side, stepped out onto the front lawn and greeted the throng.

"This is a great day," Truman said, speaking into a microphone. "This is the day we have been looking for. . . . This is the day when **fascism** and police government ceases in the world. This is the day for democracies. This is the day when we can start our real task of implementation of free government in the world."

Cheers rang out and echoed down Pennsylvania Avenue. Across the nation people danced. Cars dragged tin cans behind bumpers. People waved flags. Strangers in New York City kissed. San Francisco burned with celebratory bonfires. In Seattle, a sailor was walking down the street with his girlfriend when someone asked him about his plans for the future. "Raise babies and keep house," the sailor answered.

Just three months before, a similar scene of jubilation spread across Europe after Nazi Germany surrendered to the Allied nations led by Great Britain, the United States, and the Soviet Union. Yes, the war was over, but within a short time, the grave realities of a conflict that killed some 60 million people and devastated much of the world had set in. The war had stopped, but not the dying. Civil wars raged in China and Greece. The Soviet Union began its oppressive domination of Eastern Europe. Africa, Asia, and the Middle East exploded in conflict as European colonies shook off the shackles of their colonial rulers in **nationalistic** wars of liberation.

WHAT IS CULTURE?

Culture is often defined as a way of life for an entire society. It is reflected in a wide range of ways: by how people dress and how they speak, what movies they see, and what food they eat.

This book looks at three essential elements of culture—values, norms, and artifacts—and how each pertained to the postwar world. Values are the ideas that people believe are important. Norms are the standard patterns of behavior considered normal in a society. Artifacts are the materials, such as books, movies, and music, among others, born out of shared values and norms. Each of these elements played an essential role in the anxieties, frustrations, successes, joys, and social beliefs that defined the Cold War.

Japanese poster for the movie *Godzilla Raids Again*, 1955. Science fiction, in both books and film, represented people's anxiety about the Atomic Age.

Moreover, World War II had turned cities across much of Europe into rubble. Bombs and artillery obliterated factories, rail links, and schools. There was no water, no sanitation facilities, no place to live. Lawlessness prevailed. Bands of outlaws with weapons roamed the streets. Women prostituted themselves so they could eat. Thousands starved to death. Millions more, their homes and families destroyed, became refugees. Each looked to start a new, more secure life somewhere else. The future looked even grimmer in the Japanese cities of Hiroshima and Nagasaki, both of which were devastated by the atomic bombs dropped by the Allies at the end of the war.

Yet, amid the destruction, a new world order was slowly taking shape, one that would eventually plunge the planet into a more ideologically driven conflict between the Western democracies and communism: the Cold War. This conflict would manifest itself in many ways, including culturally. From the music people listened to and the books they read, to the values they held as a people, and to how societies and economies were organized—the Cold War was all-encompassing.

Culture and the Atomic Age

On August 6, 1945, an American B-29 bomber named the *Enola Gay* dropped the world's first atomic bomb on the Japanese city of Hiroshima. Three days later, another American atomic bomb was dropped on Nagasaki. Within that week, the Atomic Age was born. For more than four decades, the threat of nuclear **annihilation** and the fear of a growing Cold War would play a revolutionary role in literature, music, the movies, and art.

In the immediate aftermath of the nuclear blasts, some people, including many scientists, protested the proliferation of nuclear weapons. However, their protests were often drowned out by others who encouraged the West to formulate a **consensus** as it battled communism. Nevertheless, dissent arose as writers, filmmakers, musicians, and others expressed their anger and anxiety through their art.

Much of that fear could be seen in the era's science fiction movies, where filmmakers expressed anxiety about the possibility of nuclear destruction, the threat posed by communism, and the impact of radioactive fallout. These and other issues showed up in sci-fi movies in all sorts of ways: through obsessed mad scientists, invasions by aliens from outer space, and by giant mutant ants, grasshoppers, and other monsters unleashed by nuclear radiation. In Japan, which had suffered greatly because of the atomic bomb, filmmakers created a series of antinuclear films, including one called *Gojira*, or *Godzilla*. When the movie was shown in Japanese theaters, many people silently watched while others cried.

Other movies and books, including *Fail-Safe* and *Dr. Strangelove*, highlighted Cold War tensions and anxieties. In addition, the anger and angst of the age also gave voice to new poets and rock 'n' roll musicians, many of whom are discussed in the chapters that follow. New forms of culture, such as film noir (movies marked by pessimism, distrust, and **fatalism**) and others, also sprang from the nuclear age. Such "nontraditional forms of culture created in the atomic age conformed to the disorder of the age," historian Margot A. Henriksen writes in her book *Dr. Strangelove's America: Society and Culture in the Atomic Age*.

More Connected

Despite the tension and anxiety prevalent in the world, something else was occurring. A more culturally, politically, and economically connected world was emerging. The United States was the only major power that came out of the conflict virtually intact. For the time being, America was the only superpower, and its leaders envisioned a postwar world of free trade and open markets. Free markets, the Americans and their allies believed, would forge international connections that would keep the peace, spur democracy, and bring people together on economic and cultural levels.

This interconnectedness haltingly began during the war as soldiers and civilians from different cultures came together on each side of the conflict. They explored

FILM OF PROTEST

In 1959, French filmmaker Alain Resnais directed a critically acclaimed movie called *Hiroshima Mon Amour (Hiroshima My Love)*. The film focused on a French actress who travels to Hiroshima to film an antiwar movie. While in the rebuilt city, the actress, played by Emmanuelle Riva, has an affair with a Japanese architect who lost his family in the atomic blast that devastated the city.

As the two lovers talk about the effects of the blast, they begin to recall previous romances, including the woman's relationship with a German soldier during the Nazi occupation of France. The film, which uses archival footage of Hiroshima after the blast, contrasts the couple's personal pain with the devastation wrought by the bomb. The film was a success and paved the way for others in the French New Wave, a type of dramatic filmmaking that used elements of a documentary.

Many Americans of Japanese descent were taken to internment camps during World War II. However, some worked in the U.S. military as interpreters, a service much needed for operations in East Asia. Here are interpreters Herbert Miyasaki, on the left, and Akiji Yoshima, on the right, with Brigadier General Frank Merrill, who was commander of infantry troops in Burma.

places they had never seen before and interacted with people they normally would not have met. These relationships created an overarching worldview for many. Each person shared his or her personal stories and traditions, triumphs and tragedies. While some could not wait to return home, others relished these new experiences.

The war had also fostered a resurgent interest in Asia, especially East Asia, which had been brutalized by the Japanese. The Austrian mountaineer and explorer Heinrich Harrer—who gained fame in 1939 as part of the first team to ascend the north face of the Eiger in Switzerland—helped raise this renewed awareness in his book *Seven Years in Tibet*.

When the war began, the British captured Harrer on a climbing expedition in what is today Pakistan. Harrer eventually escaped and traveled to Tibet, where he became an advisor and tutor to the ten-year-old Dalai Lama. Harrer's chronicle about his life in Tibet and with the Dalai Lama, the spiritual leader of Tibetan Buddhists, underscored that even though war had made the world a much smaller place, certain parts remained free and undiscovered.

The Role of the Media

The media played a major role, both during and after the war, in forging connections and influencing universal views of humanity. The popularity of "Lili Marleen," a song based on a poem written by a German soldier in World War I, for example, transcended politics. Recorded in both German and English, the love ballad was immensely popular among Allied and German forces. It was even used for **propaganda** purposes: Marlene Dietrich, a much-loved German-American singer and film star, recorded a version used by the U.S. Office of Strategic Services to dishearten German soldiers missing their home during the war.

At home, the media shaped attitudes about the war. Americans, for example, keenly followed what was happening on the battlefield by listening to radio broadcasts, reading about it in newspapers, and watching newsreels at local theaters. These sources were key in connecting the home front to the battle front.

Although the U.S. government censored reports coming from Europe and the Pacific with a heavy hand, war correspondents traveling with the troops were able to tell the soldiers' stories. Ernie Pyle was one of the most famous. Pyle tried his best to recount the personal details of individual GIs, bringing the war home in vivid detail.

"I was at the foot of the mule trail the night they brought Capt. Waskow's body down," Pyle wrote from Italy on January 10, 1944. "The moon was nearly full at the time, and you could see far up the trail. . . . Dead men had been coming down the mountain all evening, lashed onto the backs of mules. They came lying belly-down across wooden pack-saddles, their heads hanging down on the left side of the mule."

Newspapers—there were more than 10,000 of them in the United States at the time—were not the only sources of news. Every night families sat around the radio and listened to accounts of what was happening thousands of miles away. Still

IN THEIR OWN WORDS

Austrian Explorer Heinrich Harrer

Wherever I live, I shall feel homesick for Tibet. I often think I can still hear the cries of wild geese and cranes and the beating of their wings as they fly over Lhasa in the clear, cold moonlight. My heartfelt wish is that my story may create some understanding for a people whose will to live in peace and freedom has won so little sympathy from an indifferent world.

– From *Seven Years in Tibet* (1952).

A young Marlene Dietrich, whose recording of "Lili Marleen" was widely heard by soldiers on both sides of World War II.

photographs, published in magazines such as *Life*, illustrated the horrors of war in both color and black and white.

The war hit home at every level, not only in the United States but around the world. The media brought to the world's attention the horrors of the Holocaust, the systematic murder of millions of Jews and others by the Nazis. The first reports came in August 1944, when the Soviet Red Army began liberating Nazi death camps in Eastern Europe, including Auschwitz and Treblinka.

Reporters in Asia later brought the world tales about the mistreatment of Japanese prisoners of war and female civilians in China, Korea, and the Philippines.

Both radio and newspapers were indispensable ways of getting information about the war. Pictured here is a women at Arlington Farms, Virginia, a residence for women working for the U.S. government during the war.

News would later leak out about Soviet atrocities against German women and the murder of Nazi prisoners by the French Resistance. Accounts of war crime trials in Europe and Japan shocked the world. As a result, many people reshaped their attitudes about life, humanity, dignity, war, and peace.

Uniting Nations?

The war also made the world more politically connected. It had forged an alliance between the Western democracies and the communist Soviet Union. When the war ended with the defeat of Germany and Japan, the victorious Allied nations formed the United Nations to ensure that nothing so cataclysmic would happen again. The goals of the organization were to maintain international peace and promote social progress.

The organization's charter, adopted in 1945, enshrined the concept of universal humanity. The members of the organization agreed that everyone had a right to food, shelter, and other basic freedoms. To that end, the UN in 1948 adopted the Universal Declaration of Human Rights (UDHR), intended to guide the actions of the organization and its member countries. The document provided an outline of basic human rights, including freedom of religion. "All human beings are born free and equal in dignity and rights," Article I begins. "They are endowed with reason and conscience and should act toward one another in a spirit of brotherhood." The UDHR included rights to life, liberty, and property. People should no longer be arrested without just cause or be tortured as they had been during the war. People have the right to think freely and express themselves.

To enhance the idea of basic human rights outlined in the UDHR, the UN General Assembly began to consider two additional agreements in 1954: the International Covenant on Civil and Political Rights (ICCPR) and the International Covenant on Economic, Social and Cultural Rights (ICESCR). Both were adopted in 1966. The ICESCR stipulated that all people have the right to self-determination and can pursue their own economic, social, and cultural development.

Despite the best efforts of the UN and others, the years immediately following the surrender of Germany and Japan became as perilous and as dangerous as any time in human history. The Soviets and the West each had their own vision of what a postwar world should look like. Each of those visions would manifest itself in the culture of the time.

Entrance to the United Nations Office at Geneva, in Switzerland, one of the centers of the UN's diplomatic work.

Text-Dependent Questions

1. When did the United States enter World War II?

2. Who wrote *Seven Years in Tibet*?

3. Describe the role the media played in shaping the world's view of humanity.

Research Projects

1. Use the Internet or the library to look for pictures of Americans or Europeans celebrating the end of World War II. Use one of the pictures as a guide and write a news article describing the image.

2. Research the life of Ernie Pyle or Heinrich Harrer and write a short biography covering his life during and after the war, with a section on his influence and legacy.

Educational Videos

Hiroshima: Dropping the Bomb
Page 10
An excerpt from the BBC series on Hiroshima, including first-hand accounts and dramatic recreations.

Published on YouTube by BBC Worldwide.
https://www.youtube.com/watch?v=NF4LQaWJRDg.

Ernie Pyle
Page 13
A short film on the life and work of the American WWII reporter Ernie Pyle, who died in action in Japan at the end of the war.

Published on YouTube by FranciscoProject.
https://youtu.be/zb31gk-51Co.

A 1960 advertisement for a pocket radio, built by Motorola. Small handheld radios helped to spread news, music, and other cultural "artifacts" across the airwaves in the 1950s and 1960s.

WORDS TO UNDERSTAND

dissident: relating to disagreement with the established polices or ideas of a political system.

geopolitical: relating to relationships between countries based on how they control territory.

inoculate: to create immunity to.

liberalized: relating to open economies and free markets.

satirized: ridiculed with sarcasm.

CHAPTER
2

Culture and the Cold War: 1950s and 1960s

The Cold War was not typical of other **geopolitical** conflicts in human history. Instead of being fought with guns and bombs, the Cold War was fought with ideologies and ideas and on many fronts, not the least of which were dance floors, sporting arenas, bookstores, and movie theaters. The communists used culture to push their idea that a planned economic, social, and political system was superior to the more **liberalized**, market-oriented Western democracies.

In the years immediately following World War II, popular culture in both the Western and communist worlds mirrored the anxiety each side felt as the threat of nuclear war hung over the planet. Each side used culture as a weapon to promote its respective way of life. They did this not only in search of new global allies, but also in their own societies, where many people had opposing viewpoints or were interested in the other side's ideas and way of life. Highlighting and promoting each culture was a form of propaganda, a way for both sides to win approval for their political and economic agendas. Both sides used art exhibitions, sporting events, ballet, books, fine arts, music, and movies as if they were bombs and airplanes.

Congress for Cultural Freedom

During the grueling years of the Great Depression, well into the 1930s, many people in the West and elsewhere had become desperate. Their economic hardship ground on, with little sign of recovery. To many, capitalism seemed to have lost its credibility as a viable economic system, and the planned Soviet system seemed to hold more promise and stability.

This view persisted beyond World War II, even as economic recovery was in hand. Given growing concern about the influence of the communist ideas in the early years of the Cold War, the United States decided to commit a lot of time, money, and personnel to, in the words of historian Frances Stonor Saunders, "**inoculate** the world against the contagion of Communism and to ease the passage of American foreign policy interests abroad."

One of the most ambitious parts of that plan was the formation of the Congress for Cultural Freedom (CCF), which used writers, poets, artists, and others to counter the worldview put forth by the Soviet Union. It aimed to convince potential doubters that liberal democracy was much better than the Soviet model of "command and control," of planned economic, cultural, and social systems. The CCF was established in 1950, one year after the Cultural and Scientific Conference for World Peace in New York City caused a stir. At the conference, a group of 800 intellectuals, artists, writers, and others, along with Soviet delegates, met at the Waldorf Astoria Hotel to urge the West to make peace with the Soviet Union. The group, which included playwright Arthur Miller, writer Norman Mailer, and composer Aaron Copland, slammed the United States for "warmongering."

Russian composer Dmitri Shostakovich, an official Soviet delegate to the conference, urged the Americans to get along with Russia. Shostakovich's words resonated with playwright Clifford Odets. Odets claimed that the American government was spreading false reports of Soviet intentions and had created a "state of holy terror" in the United States. For his part, Copland said, "the present policies of the American government will lead inevitably into a third world war."

As Odets, Copland, and the others railed against the United States, another group, the anticommunist Americans for Intellectual Freedom, voiced a much different view of the world at the conference. In Washington, government officials saw what was going on in New York and wondered how anticommunist intellectuals could help counter the Soviet cultural propaganda machine.

When the Congress for Cultural Freedom was established in 1950, it was subsidized secretly by America's spy agency, the CIA. The U.S. Congress went to work sending symphonies on tours of Europe and helping to fund artists and writers—many without their knowledge. The Congress hosted dozens of conferences, published magazines, and held art shows.

The Soviets were not to be outdone. Stalin's government actively promoted classics of Soviet literature, theater,

Dmitri Shostakovich, official Soviet delegate to the 1949 peace conference in New York City. A world-renowned composer, he joined U.S. intellectuals and artists in urging the Soviets and Americans to work toward peace.

Lyudmila Semenyaka and Nikolai Kovmir performing at the Soviet Union's first international ballet competition, in Moscow in 1969.

music, and ballet. The Soviets sent symphonies, ice shows, circuses, and dance troupes to tour throughout the West. According to historian and U.S. foreign service officer Yale Richmond, between 1958 and 1988, more than 50,000 Soviet scholars, students, writers, musicians, dancers, and others came to the United States. Soviet leaders were determined to draw a stark contrast to the capitalist West by showing that communism respected culture over material wealth.

Consumer Culture

The clash of cultures played out in the aisles of department stores, new-car lots, and grocery stores across the Western world. As the Cold War began, so did a new era in consumerism—the belief that personal consumption of material goods is a sign of economic health and strength. Abetted by the explosion of public relations and advertising, the economies of the West—first in the United States and later elsewhere—overflowed with new products. New cars, televisions, washing machines, toasters, and ovens began to define contemporary living. Advertising was the oil that greased the free market machine, fueling consumerism and creating a demand for more products.

The middle class in the United States was a prime audience. Before the war, much of the world, including the United States, was mired in the Great Depression, when people only bought the necessities. They rarely took out loans because they feared being in debt. Their economic condition during the era was often perilous.

A young Italian boy poses with his family's television set, circa 1950.

But after the war, economic doubt began to melt away. Veterans returned from the war and began working. Many went to college under the government-funded GI Bill. As prosperity increased, banks made it easier for people to obtain credit. Attitudes began to change and cash registers began to ring. People started to buy new homes, new cars, and new appliances.

Although consumerism took hold first in the United States, it wouldn't be long before Japan and Western Europe followed, spurred on by rapid reconstruction and the redevelopment of each nation's economic system. For example, West Germany's "economic miracle," known as Wirtschaftswunder, was in full swing by the mid-to-late 1950s and became so tantalizing for Germans living in communist East Germany that many fled for the West through Berlin.

Yet, after a time, many people began to recoil from this high-flying consumerism. Writers such as J. D. Salinger railed against conformity created by material wealth and consumerism. Artist Andy Warhol, who had helped fuel the new age of consumerism as an advertising illustrator in the 1950s, **satirized** Western consumer culture by creating repeating images of soup cans and soda bottles. Warhol, a master of irony, once painted a dented soup can with a peeling label in his attempt to question the conformity typical of consumer-driven societies.

The Kitchen Debate

Nothing showed how important consumerism was during the Cold War as much as the so-called Kitchen Debate between U.S. vice president Richard Nixon and Soviet premier Nikita Khrushchev. On July 24, 1959, the two men got into a pointed argument about capitalism versus communism at a model kitchen set up for the American National Exhibition in Moscow. This exhibition followed another in New York City of Soviet culture a month earlier.

Nixon, an ardent anticommunist, celebrated the free market by showing Khrushchev dishwashers and other appliances. The Soviet leader, never one to back down from a confrontation, dismissed Western technology, saying that Soviet factories would soon be producing better products.

"The Americans have created their own image of the Soviet man. But he is not as you think," Khrushchev told Nixon. "You think the Russian people will be dumbfounded to see these things, but the fact is that newly built Russian houses have all this equipment right now."

Nixon shot back: "This exhibit was not designed to astound but to interest. Diversity, the right to choose, the fact that we have one thousand builders building one thousand different houses is the most important thing. We don't have one decision made at the top by one government official. This is the difference."

In July 1959, U.S. vice president Richard Nixon and Soviet premier Nikita Khrushchev debate consumer culture and lifestyle, as they view a reproduction of an American kitchen at the American National Exhibition in Moscow. The clash came to be known as the "Kitchen Debate."

The Rise of Television

January 19, 1953, was must-see TV in the United States. Lucille Ball and her real-life husband, Desi Arnaz, were about to have a baby. The two had been starring in the popular television show *I Love Lucy*. Viewers had followed Lucy's pregnancy throughout the year. Finally, on January 19, viewers tuned in as Lucy went to the hospital to give birth. Although the show had been filmed earlier, some 44 million people parked themselves in front of their TV sets. When the show was over, people sent Ball nearly a million cards, telegrams, and gifts.

I Love Lucy was so popular that people stayed home each Monday night to watch the show. Even the Chicago department store Marshall Field & Co. hung out a sign that said, "We Love Lucy too, so we're closing on Monday nights." Although television had been around for a while, it wasn't until the late 1950s that it had become the most popular household fixture. In 1946 there were about 8,000 television sets in the United States. Eleven years later, there were 40 million.

Television opened a new world of entertainment and allowed people to see what different cultures were like. As people all around the world watched, they became intrigued with other nations. Many liked what they saw and moved to other regions of the world in search of new economic opportunity. Moreover, people in rural areas began to move into urban centers. Television also introduced new ideas and expanded access to news and information. It often spurred people to action. Reading about starving children or a far-off war was one thing, but actually seeing the misery was something much different.

Yet, most American television programs in the 1950s depicted a narrow view of life. TV families did not face economic problems. There were few, if any, African Americans, Hispanics (except for Desi Arnaz's Ricky Ricardo), or other minority characters. Instead, most shows, such as *The Adventures of Ozzie and Harriet* and *Father Knows Best*, centered on white, middle-class, suburban families. These shows portrayed females as stay-at-home moms and males as bread-winning dads, reinforcing widely accepted gender roles.

"What type of girl would you have Wally marry?" Ward Cleaver asked his wife, June, during

Lucille Ball and Desi Arnaz, stars of the popular American TV show *I Love Lucy*. Arnaz—Lucille Ball's real-life, and on-screen, husband—was one of the first Hispanic Americans to star in a television series.

Yuri Gagarin, the Soviet cosmonaut who was the first human to enter outer space, in 1961. Television helped to establish him as a hero of the communist world after his return to Earth was captured on TV. Here, he receives a hero's welcome in Warsaw, Poland, in 1961.

an episode of *Leave It to Beaver.* "Oh," she answered, "some very sensible girl from a nice family . . . one . . . who's a good cook and can keep a nice house, and see that he's happy."

Despite the obvious dissonance between reality and TV, television had also become a galvanizing medium. TV brought home the battle for civil rights and gave people a front-row seat to the escalating tensions between the Soviet Union and the United States. TV also followed American astronauts as they blasted off into space for the first time.

Communist officials in Europe liked television because it could bring their vision of culture to the masses. For the communist world, as well as the West, TV was used as a propaganda tool. When cosmonaut Yuri Gagarin returned to Earth in 1961, after becoming the first human in space, his welcome home celebration was widely televised, not only in the Soviet Union but in other countries, including Sweden and the Netherlands.

Oppressive Media

Unlike the West, the media in the Soviet Bloc was strictly controlled by the state. After the Russian Revolution in 1917, the newly formed Communist Party under Vladimir Lenin took control of all media to paint a positive image of his regime. The media never deviated from Lenin's script. Over the years, Soviet leaders continued to restrict free expression. The Russian people, generally, saw, read, and heard what the state allowed. Those who attempted to gain information any other way, such as through the U.S.–funded Voice of America, which broadcast news from outside the Soviet Bloc, were severely punished.

Soviet premier Joseph Stalin was a master of media. He used all types to his advantage. Artists painted flattering portraits of the dictator. Photographers took pictures of Stalin in white suits so he stood out among everyone else. The media formulated an image of Stalin as "Uncle Joe," the "father" of all Russians. Writers and poets were expected to toe the party line.

Yet the authoritarian Soviet system could not silence **dissident** writers, and intellectuals wrote critically about communism. The dissidents were either jailed or branded as mentally ill. Many were sent to gulags—Soviet labors camps. As a result, literature went underground. Writers called these banned writings *samizdat.*

1984

One of the most important writings to come out of the Cold War was George Orwell's *1984*. Inspired by the rise of totalitarian dictators such as Adolf Hitler in Germany and Stalin in the Soviet Union, *1984* was a politically charged novel that took a harsh look at authoritarian governments and the totalitarianism impulse in general. Published in 1949, *1984* was Orwell's warning of what could happen in totalitarian and other societies whose governments became too powerful. It depicted a post-atomic world in which a dictatorship monitored the activities of every citizen.

View from Africa

On October 1, 1960, the British flag that had flown high over Nigeria since the 1850s was pulled down. In its place, the green and white flag of the newly independent country of Nigeria was unfurled. There had been just four independent nations in Africa five years after World War II ended. By the end of 1960—Africa's "Year of Freedom"—there were twenty-seven. Seventeen of these, including Nigeria, had gained their independence during that year.

After the war, the influence of the great European colonial powers began to wane in Africa, Asia, the Americas, and the Middle East. The war had substantially weakened the old colonial powers to the point where their claims of cultural, racial, and economic superiority were discredited. Although many of these colonies ultimately won independence through negotiation or wars of national liberation, the legacy of colonialism often remained. Many newly minted African nations were tossed into a seemingly never-ending series of conflicts, fueled by racial, ethnic, linguistic, religious, and cultural differences. Moreover, both the Soviet Union and United States attempted to shape the politics of these new states and guide them into their orbits.

While many African leaders worked to shape the political and economic future of their countries, others tried to guide each nation's cultural identity. Many writers, poets, and journalists used the typewriter and the printing press to establish their cultural independence. These individuals were not only artists but also political activists. Much of their early work focused on freedom and hope. As many African nations struggled to govern themselves, their work became more desperate and angry. Writers railed not only against their old colonial masters but also against the corrupt leaders who replaced them.

In 1966 a small group of "linguistic guerrillas" in Morocco published a literary journal called *Souffles*. Founded by the Moroccan poet Abdellatif Laâbi, the magazine gave writers, artists, and intellectuals an alternative outlet. In it, they were encouraged to experiment in ways that diverged from the traditional literary world—one that they claimed was dominated by the attitudes and culture of former colonial powers. The government banned the magazine in 1972 and arrested Laâbi, who was freed in 1980. The magazine expressed the angst that many of those in the postcolonial Third World felt.

Souffles was not the only publication that articulated the dehumanizing effects of colonization. In 1961 Frantz Fanon, a psychiatrist born on the Caribbean island of Martinique, published *The Wretched of the Earth*, an analysis of how colonization impacted the psychological health of individuals. *The Wretched of the Earth* gave voice to the frustration of colonized peoples and the role violence plays in effecting change. In addition to his work as a psychiatrist, Fanon supported national liberation movements, including the one in Algeria, where he lived later in life.

THE CULTURAL DIVIDE

Religion and language were often at the center of postcolonial conflicts. When the Europeans colonized Africa, for example, they brought with them their religion–Christianity. The Europeans tried to convert as many people as they could. Occasionally, Africans mixed aspects of Western religion with traditional beliefs, creating new religions.

Many Africans also followed Islam, a religion brought to the continent by Arab traders during the Middle Ages. In many cases, the borders of the newly independent nations did not take into account the rivalry between religious groups, nor did they take into account differences in languages, cultures, and ethnic allegiances. Groups who had hated each other for centuries were suddenly given the task of nation-building. These differences often led to political instability and war.

Moroccan poet Abdellatif Laâbi in 2011.

The tomb of Frantz Fanon in Algeria.

Changes were taking place not just in Africa, but in other regions as well. After the successful 1949 Chinese Communist Revolution, for instance, Mao Zedong sought to have China reassert itself as a great civilization that had been weakened by Western imperialists. He worked to modernize China by promoting the status of women and providing health care and education to the masses. Writers used fictionalized stories, poetry, drama, and opera to promote Mao's ideology. The state rewarded many writers, performers, and artists, at least those who promoted the party line. Mao believed the arts were essential to the success of communism.

In India, nationalistic literature played an important role in that country's struggle for independence. Many texts not only centered on the politics of India's nationalistic leaders, but also questioned the path India should take once it was free from British rule. Other stories, such as those written by Mulk Raj Anand, focused on the urban poor, who had been downtrodden and weakened under colonialism.

Text-Dependent Questions

1. When was the Kitchen Debate held?
2. Which year was Africa's "Year of Freedom"?
3. Describe the importance of the samizdat.

Research Projects

1. Look at the "Lessons by Artwork" page on the Warhol website (http://www.warhol.org/education/resourceslessons/lessonsby-artwork/) to examine the artwork of Andy Warhol. Pick three or four images that you like or dislike and explain to the class why you feel that way.

2. Read the first few pages of George Orwell's *1984*, which can be found in your library or on the Internet (one source is https://archive.org/details/Orwell1984preywo). Write a short essay—of two or three paragraphs—describing your understanding of and reaction to "BIG BROTHER."

Educational Video

The Kitchen Debate
Page 23
News footage of U.S. vice president Richard Nixon in a friendly confrontation with Soviet premier Nikita Khrushchev, on July 24, 1959.

Published on YouTube by the Richard Nixon Foundation.

https://youtu.be/XRgOz2x9c08.

WORDS TO UNDERSTAND

automatons: people who act like machines.

bourgeois: having qualities or values associated with the middle class.

conformity: condition of being similar to others in thoughts and values.

paranoia: unreasonable fear, suspicion, or distrust.

ABOVE: Young Americans, black and white, from Riverhead High School in 1962, enjoying the music and doing "the twist," a new dance craze, as they travel by train to Montauk, Long Island, in New York State.

The Counterculture and East Meets West: 1960s

The 1950s were dominated by a generation tempered first by economic calamity during the Great Depression, and by later a world war. When the fighting ended and prosperity returned, **conformity** and conventionality were welcomed respites. Westerners, especially Americans, had more money to buy the things that had eluded them for decades. Home ownership spiked. New cars, new refrigerators, new TVs, and new hi-fi systems filled store shelves, living rooms, garages, and kitchens. Women who had worked during the war left their jobs and renewed their traditional roles as housewives and mothers.

Filmmakers and writers, such as Sloan Wilson, captured the triviality and predictability of the era. "I really don't know what I was looking for when I got back from the war, but it seemed as though all I could see was a lot of bright young men in gray flannel suits rushing around New York in a frantic parade to nowhere," Wilson wrote in his novel *The Man in the Gray Flannel Suit*. "They seemed to me to be pursuing neither ideals nor happiness—they were pursuing a routine. . . . It was quite a shock to glance down and see that I too was wearing a gray flannel suit."

By the beginning of the 1960s, however, that questioning of the status quo began to take hold. In the United States, black music and beatniks were influencing a generation of young people, the civil rights movement was beginning to press for equal rights for African Americans, and women started to look for satisfaction beyond their homes. Similar trends began to be seen around the world—the 1960s were a time of change.

A Soviet Thaw

In the Soviet Union, while the "man in the gray flannel suit" lamented his postwar fate, the mid-1950s ushered in a new, more promising era in the Soviet Union, thanks to a thaw under Nikita Khrushchev. At the time, the Soviet premier relaxed the government's repressive stance, giving rise to a sense of optimism among writers, artists, and intellectuals. This new optimistic outlook affected a young Mikhail Gorbachev,

ALEKSANDR SOLZHENITSYN

One of the most famous dissident writers in the Soviet Union was Aleksandr Solzhenitsyn, who wrote *One Day in the Life of Ivan Denisovich*, a novel about life in a Soviet labor camp. Under Khrushchev's cultural thaw, the government allowed it to be published in 1962. The novel was an extraordinary event in the Soviet Union. Until then, no account of Soviet repression had ever been widely disseminated. Solzhenitsyn later went on to write *The Gulag Archipelago*, in which he described the horrors of the Soviet labor camps. The book was a sensation in many countries, but the Soviet government stripped Solzhenitsyn of his citizenship. They imprisoned him and later sent him into exile.

Aleksandr Solzhenitsyn, one of the Soviet Union's most famous dissidents. He wrote *One Day in the Life of Ivan Denisovich*, which was published in the Soviet Union during the "Khrushchev Thaw."

who some years later would foster democratization in the Soviet political and economic systems.

Khrushchev initiated the thaw in 1953 upon the death of Stalin. He quickly denounced the brutal Soviet dictator and ousted his supporters from government. Russian writers, whose voices Stalin had silenced for decades, began to publish again. It was during this period that Aleksandr Solzhenitsyn's novel *One Day in the Life of Ivan Denisovich*, saw publication, in 1962 (see sidebar). The thaw could be seen in other media as well. Foreign films were allowed in theaters, and television introduced variety and comedy shows for broadcast. Western democratic ideas, in small ways, began to influence the curriculum at Soviet universities.

Although Khrushchev periodically tightened the reigns on cultural expression and political freedom, the general trend during his rule was to loosen the iron grip on Soviet cultural life. While the "Khrushchev Thaw" ended in 1964 when the premier was ousted from power, his more open policies sowed seeds of change that eventually bore fruit in the 1980s, when politicians such as Gorbachev came to power.

A Much More Dangerous Place

Although each side in the Cold War had reasons to be optimistic, the world was still a dangerous place. Communism expanded into Asia and Eastern Europe, subjugating country after country. The United States countered by offering military and economic support to pro-Western governments in Africa, Southeast Asia, Latin America, and the Middle East.

A display in an Italian museum of the film *The Wild One*, starring Marlon Brando, who played Johnny Strabler, the head of a motorcycle gang. By the late 1950s, outlaw motorcycle gangs—who rebelled against all aspects of traditional society—had an iconic status in American culture, one that eventually spread across international borders.

Paranoia over "the red menace" drove political witch hunts. The specter of nuclear annihilation was more than real. Poverty was epidemic, not only in inner cities but also in rural regions such as Appalachia. Women, African Americans, Mexican migrants, and Native Americans struggled for basic civil rights. Nationalistic movements gained traction in Africa and Asia, destabilizing both regions.

Younger people slowly began to scrutinize the direction the West was moving. Many did not like what they saw. Some began to rebel against conformity and the politics of consensus to develop a culture of their own—a counterculture—one that contradicted the existing conservative political and social norms.

"Hey Johnny, what are you rebelling against?" a woman asks Marlon Brando's character in the 1953 movie, *The Wild One*, after she notices a motorcycle club jacket on one of Brando's friends. "Whadda you got?" he answers.

Influence of the Beat Generation

A group of writers and thinkers in the 1950s railed against the blandness of middle-class life. Known as the "Beats," Jack Kerouac, Allen Ginsberg, and others blasted the conformity of the age. They criticized suburbia, materialism, and denounced politicians.

The Beats sought intellectual and economic freedom—the freedom to go anywhere and to do anything. They saw themselves as outliers in a land of **automatons**.

They embraced drugs, sex, and music. Inspired by jazz and its culture, the Beats dressed in dark clothes and used a "hipster" vernacular that they created. "Money" was "bread," "wonderful" was "cool," and to be "hip" was to "understand." Their protests, their writings, their music, their very language added to a cultural revolution that would engulf much of the Western world.

According to historian Jeremi Suri in "The Rise and Fall of an International Counterculture, 1960–1975," published in 2009, "Existential angst was not unique to the period, but it became pervasive in a context of heightened promises about a better life and strong fears about the political implications of social deviance. Ideological competition in the Cold War encouraged citizens to look beyond material factors alone, and to seek a deeper meaning in their daily activities."

The Beats preached that postwar life was tedious, dull, and boring, and a receptive young audience took note. They began to see sexuality, drugs, gender roles, and authority in a different light. Some of what the Beats wrote was dark, which mimicked other forms of art. Brando's *The Wild One*, in which he played the leader of a motorcycle gang, for instance, fascinated the young, while terrifying their parents.

Unlike their parents, the youth inspired by the Beats grew up in an era of material wealth and did not have to fret about life's necessities. The kind of social criticism typical of the Beats motivated young people to focus on cultural, economic, and social inequities. Soon many younger Americans became political activists during the 1960s and 1970s, inspired especially by the civil rights movement of the 1950s and 1960s.

The band of trumpeter Dizzy Gillespie (front left), with bassist Ray Brown (at the right), John Lewis (at the piano), and a young Miles Davis (on trumpet, second from left in the back). Jazz music influenced not only the Beats in the United States, but many throughout Europe, in their quest for authenticity in the face of contemporary conformity.

Intellectuals, as well as middle-class college students in Britain and America, developed their own brand of so-called New Left politics. They criticized corporations, government, social institutions, and the way universities taught students. They used college campuses as a petri dish to foster change.

Marxist in ideology, New Left organizations such as the Students for a Democratic Society sought reforms in areas such as gay rights, women's rights, and civil rights. All of this grew in intensity in the early 1960s and expanded as the civil rights movement gained traction and the United States became more involved in an unpopular war in Vietnam. Many of the activists were wrongly inspired by Mao's bloody Cultural Revolution in China, in which the communist leader sought to reignite the revolutionary fervor that brought him to power. Attacking traditional values and **bourgeois** attitudes, young Red Guard groups led the charge, persecuting those who were insufficiently "revolutionary" in outlook.

The Global Counterculture

The growing counterculture was not just an American phenomenon, but also a global movement that found fertile ground in Western Europe. The British embraced such causes as environmentalism, gay liberation, women's rights, and nuclear disarmament. French youth also embraced the tenets of the counterculture, railing against corporations, government, and the rivalry between the West and the communists. In May 1968, student protesters took over several universities to protest the educational system, capitalism, and joblessness. The most radical called for revolution, as the protests spread to France's industrial centers and factories, effectively shutting down the national economy. In response, French president Charles de Gaulle dissolved the National Assembly and called for elections. De Gaulle, buoyed by his supporters in the middle class, rallied, and by late June the protests were over. De Gaulle's government enacted a series of reforms, including higher wages for workers and the overhaul of the nation's educational system.

West Germany was also a bastion of the counterculture, especially in the communes, where artists, writers, and left-leaning political activists gathered to live. The first, Kommune 1, was created in West Berlin in 1967 as an alternative living arrangement. The

IN THEIR OWN WORDS

Allen Ginsberg, Beat Poet

I saw the best minds of my generation destroyed by madness, starving hysterical naked, dragging themselves through the negro streets at dawn looking for an angry fix.

−From *Howl and Other Poems*, 1956.

Allen Ginsberg, 1979

A strike at a factory in the south of France in 1968, during the countrywide protest by students and workers; the poster at the left reads "Factory Occupied by Workers," and on the right is a list of their demands.

idea behind the Kommune was to expose conservative social values and change what commune members thought was an unjust social system. The communes were a wellspring of high political theater. Members of Kommune 1, for example, once planned to attack U.S. vice president Hubert Humphrey with nonlethal objects, including paint, flour, and pudding, Humphrey's favorite dessert. The "pudding assassination" never took place.

The West German counterculture movement also helped a group of teenage rockers from Liverpool, England, to hone their art: John Lennon, Paul McCartney, George Harrison, Pete Best, and Stuart Sutcliffe—the Beatles. The group arrived in Hamburg in 1961 and began to develop a unique musical style. Three years later, the Beatles became the most influential rock band in music history. They came to the United States in 1964 with new drummer Ringo Starr, but without Best and Sutcliffe, and set off on a countercultural tsunami that ripped apart conventional social norms and paved the way for other British artists, including the Rolling Stones, the Kinks, and The Who, among others.

By the late 1960s, Germany's rock musicians had developed a style of their own, fusing psychedelic rock (inspired by hallucinogenic drugs) with electronic sounds. The Krautrock movement, as it was called, would later influence New Age artists,

A tribute to the Beatles on a corner in Hamburg, 2010.

alternative rock, and a type of rock music that developed out of the post-punk genre of the 1970s.

Rock 'n' roll was one of the top cultural commodities in an ever-growing globalized world. Rock gave voice to a younger generation that was worried about many things. Folk music did the same. Artists—such as Bob Dylan; Joan Baez; Peter, Paul and Mary; and Simon and Garfunkel—sang with homespun clarity about the impoverished, the marginalized, and the disenfranchised. Their music was a call to action. They recorded songs against the morality of the times, inspiring millions to stand up to the authoritarian class that included politicians, police, and parents.

Music also spurred the publication of the underground press in many countries, including Great Britain, the United States, and France—even in India, Bangladesh, and other developing countries. The underground press, also known as the alternative press, focused attention on culture, social issues, and left-wing politics. Most of these papers were printed weeklies or monthlies that analyzed issues from a progressive perspective; most were free. In some nations, these newspapers and magazines were illegal and were often shut down by the government because they challenged the status quo.

East Meets West

During the 1960s and 1970s, something spiritually unifying was happening, as the West became more aware of Eastern culture. The Beatles, who by the mid-1960s had achieved iconic cultural status, made a well-publicized trip to Rishikesh, India, to meet with the Maharishi Mahesh Yogi, who had developed a form of spirituality called Transcendental Meditation.

By the mid- to-late 1960s, the Beatles had become the de facto leaders in the counterculture movement. They tried many things, including taking hallucinogenic drugs, in the hopes of achieving a higher state of consciousness. Traveling to India was part of this quest. Guitarist George Harrison spent a lot of time in India learning how to play the sitar—a stringed instrument with a long, fretted neck—with musician Ravi Shankar.

THREE DAYS OF LOVE, PEACE, AND ROCK 'N' ROLL AT WOODSTOCK

On August 15, 1969, the Woodstock Music and Art Fair began on Max Yasgur's farm in upstate New York. Billed as three days of peace, love, and rock 'n' roll, the festival was a cultural phenomenon that resonated with the generation coming of age in the 1960s.

The festival was born because the promoters—John Roberts, Joel Rosenman, Artie Kornfeld, and Michael Lang—wanted to make enough money to build a recording studio in the town of Woodstock. When they couldn't get approval from the town to hold the festival there, they asked Yasgur to use his dairy farm in Bethel, some sixty miles away. The name Woodstock, however, stuck—the posters were already printed. Yasgur agreed. The promoters at first sold 186,000 tickets, but word quickly spread.

Hundreds of thousands of people crowded the New York State Thruway on their way to the festival. So many people arrived on the first day that the promoters decided to let everyone in free of charge. "Woodstock Nation" is a term people would use to describe the youth culture of the time.

As the Beatles became more involved in meditation, so did their fans. Transcendental Meditation centers and classes sprang up around the world. Doctors and therapists recommended that their stressed-out patients meditate. *Life* magazine called 1968 "The Year of the Guru," while the *New York Times Magazine* dubbed the Maharishi "The Chief Guru of the Western World." Millions embraced his philosophy.

Maharishi Mahesh Yogi with followers in 1979 at a university founded by the Maharishi in Iowa.

Violence and Counterculture

The counterculture fostered a new brand of left-wing politics that sometimes came into conflict with the mainstream in the most violent of ways. From the United States to Germany, to Italy, and behind the Iron Curtain, protesters clashed with the ruling elite. In August 1968, counterculture political activists in the United States, for example, clashed with police and National Guard units for five days outside the Democratic National Convention in Chicago, as they protested U.S. involvement in the Vietnam War.

One of the most profound battles occurred early in 1968 when Alexander Dubček, first secretary of the Communist Party of Czechoslovakia, granted the press greater freedoms. By April he had initiated a sweeping reform program—referred to as the Prague Spring—that included constitutional revisions that guaranteed civil rights and liberties. Dubček was confident he could control the reforms, which also included making the government more democratic. The Soviets and other members of the Warsaw Pact looked on with alarm, fearing Dubček's reforms would spread across the communist world.

On August 20, the Soviet army marched into Prague to put down what they saw as a counterrevolution. The Czechs, mostly young students, resisted peacefully for the most part. Still, clashes ensued, and seventy-two people lost their lives.

Demonstrators in Helsinki, Finland, in 1968 protesting the Soviet invasion of Czechoslovakia.

Text-Dependent Questions

1. Why were rock music and folk music important to the counterculture movement?

2. What were the "Beats" protesting?

3. Who was Maharishi Mahesh Yogi and why was he important?

Research Project

Many Beatle songs were influenced by their journeys to India, including "My Sweet Lord" and "Within You Without You," among others. Pick one of these songs and either listen to it or research the lyrics. Describe what you believe is the Eastern influence of this music.

A women's rights march in Washington, D.C., in 1970.

![reading icon]

WORDS TO UNDERSTAND

actualization: realizing and attaining one's identity and full potential.

feminists: people who support women's rights and equality.

humanitarian: relating to the promotion of social welfare and the common good of humanity.

indigenous: native.

neutered: feeling a loss of one's sexual identity and drive.

Equal Rights and the End of the Cold War: Into the 1980s

The reshaping of social and political norms, reflected in the civil rights movement and the counterculture of the 1960s, also motivated other movements of liberation. Gay rights in the United States began to take shape in 1969, after police raided the Stonewall Inn, a gay bar in New York City's Greenwich Village. Britain's first Gay Pride Rally took place in 1972 in London. Movements for the rights of **indigenous** groups, such as Native Americans and the Maori in New Zealand, also began to gather steam in the late 1960s and 1970s. Gradually, human rights were being embraced across the globe.

The Women's Movement

During this time, women started to become a dominant political and cultural force. They fought for equal pay with men, equal rights at work, reproductive rights, and laws against sexual harassment. One of the first books to explore women's lives and identities was *The Feminine Mystique* by Betty Friedan. Published in 1963, it offered messages of sexual and domestic liberation. Friedan argued that the lives of women in the postwar world were far from meaningful. She called on women to move beyond the roles of homemaker, wife, and mother.

By the 1970s, other **feminists** were arguing strenuously for women's full social and political rights, as well as self-exploration and **actualization**. Germaine Greer's *The Female Eunich* explored such themes, including how the traditional values of suburban families left wives and mothers **neutered** and lifeless. Greer's book, published originally in England in 1970, became an international bestseller, eventually being translated into eleven languages.

Germaine Greer, author of
The Female Eunich, in 1972.

Encouraged by these writings and by the era's general climate of freedom and openness, many women rebelled against the stagnation they felt as homemakers and mothers. By the 1970s, the widening use of the birth control pill—which had been approved by the U.S. Food and Drug Administration in 1960—meant that women could have sex without worrying about getting pregnant. The Pill, as it became known, allowed women to make decisions about their own bodies and welfare. They could have children when they wanted. It freed women to plan and build careers.

The feminist movement was not just about changing laws; it also sought to fundamentally shift the way society viewed, spoke about, and ultimately treated women. Magazines such as *Cosmopolitan* talked directly to women about sex and relationships. When asked to describe what the magazine was, its editor, Helen Gurley Brown, said, "Cosmo is feminist in that we believe women are just as smart and capable as men are and can achieve anything men can. But it also acknowledges that while work is important, men are too."

A More Humane World?

By the 1970s and 1980s, respect for women's rights, native rights, gay rights—in effect, human rights—had taken center stage. Global watchdog groups, such as Amnesty International and Human Rights Watch, became advocates for free speech and other peaceful protest activities, particularly for those who suffered abuse at the hands of government. As individual groups argued for increased rights and freedoms, human rights were soon seen as part of a universal **humanitarian** ideal.

SIMONE DE BEAUVOIR

One of the first books to discuss the unequal status of women was *The Second Sex* by Simone de Beauvoir, published in France in 1949 and translated into English in 1953. In *The Second Sex*, de Beauvoir argued that throughout history men had always oppressed women, whom they believed were inherently inferior.

The World Refugee Rally in Brisbane, Australia, in June 2015. The Australian senator Larissa Walters (taking notes) is marching in solidarity with members of Amnesty International, the human rights organization that, in 1977, had won the Nobel Peace Prize.

By the mid-1960s, the UN's humanitarian work had begun to intensify. In 1964 it formed the Group of 77 to help the developing world, and in 1965 it established the UN Development Programme, which began to take cultural and social factors into account when analyzing development and well-being. The organization also passed a number of treaties that further defined and elaborated on human rights, including agreements to end torture and genocide and to help refugees, women, and children. Even regional organizations in Africa and elsewhere worked to safeguard human rights.

Writers, artists, and intellectuals also worked to expand human rights in their own countries. Soviet dissidents, for example, demanded political, economic, and social reform. In Czechoslovakia, a group of writers and other intellectuals, including Václav Havel, who became the president of the Czech Republic in 1989, asked the government to recognize basic human rights through a petition known as "Charter 77." Although the document, created in 1977, was not very radical by any measure—it contained most of the rights already guaranteed by the Czech constitution—it was an important step in making a communist society more open and inclusive.

In addition, globalizing forces, which were reflected already in the spreading of the counterculture and liberation movements across borders, slowly turned the Soviet Union into a more porous society. In order to ease geopolitical tensions with the West, both sides embarked on a policy of détente, a French word that means "relaxation." Nuclear destruction was still a very real possibility during the 1970s. In order to reduce this threat and increase trade between Cold War enemies, the Soviet Union and United States worked to find common ground on many issues. Both nations signed treaties to reduce nuclear stockpiles and cooperated in scientific research, including a joint space venture in 1975. U.S. president Richard Nixon and Soviet premier Leonid Brezhnev even visited each other's country.

The spirit of détente also extended into Asia. In 1971, relations between China—the world's most populous communist nation—and the United States began to thaw when a ping-pong team from the United States visited China. It was the first time since the 1949 revolution that a group of Americans had entered the country. *Time* magazine called it the "ping heard round the world." The table tennis match began an era of "Ping-Pong Diplomacy" between the two countries. A year later, Richard Nixon, who molded his political career as an ardent anticommunist, visited China, met with Mao, and walked the Great Wall.

Crisis of Confidence

Although the Cold War was warming, by the late 1970s, economic problems created a crisis of confidence in the West. Skyrocketing oil prices, sparked by a drastic cut in oil production by the Organization of Arab Petroleum Exporting Countries (OAPEC), precipitated a worldwide depression. OAPEC had launched the oil embargo, as it was called, in response to the war between Israel, supported by the United States, and its Arab neighbors. Many felt that the West, specifically the United States, was in decline, especially after its defeat in Vietnam and President Nixon's forced resignation in 1974.

To complicate matters, Britain's economic promise was also in doubt. Not only had it lost its empire, but it also had to deal with an increasingly violent nationalistic movement in Northern Ireland. Marxist-inspired movements spread across several other European countries. But not all was in turmoil. Germany had become an economic powerhouse, and China was slowly opening its society after the death of Mao in 1976.

Yet something else was occurring during this period that would have profound consequences throughout the world: the Soviet economy had begun to implode, as it was unable to meet the demands of its military and citizens. In 1985 Mikhail

LEFT: Václav Havel (at right) at the monument in Prague to the Velvet Revolution, a peaceful transition from Soviet-backed dictatorship to democracy in 1989. Havel became the president of the Czech Republic after the Velvet Revolution. He was also one of the leaders in drafting the human rights document Charter 77, in 1977.

Germans remove pieces of the Berlin Wall as souvenirs following the reunification of East and West Berlin.

Gorbachev came to power and began to reform the Soviet system, hoping to make it more open. He also encouraged other Eastern European countries to do the same. By 1989 the Berlin Wall, which separated communist East Berlin from West Berlin and was long a symbol of Cold War tensions, was torn down. Two years later, the Soviet Union had collapsed. The Cold War was over.

The Last Superpower?

The United States was now the last superpower standing. Its liberal economic, social, cultural, and political ideologies had outperformed the Soviet system, and some other nations adopted American capitalist practices as the best path forward. The Cold War's end also meant that the United States no longer had a powerful adversary. Just what its role in this "New World Order" would be was uncertain, to say the least.

After World War II, the West, led by the United States, asserted capitalist dominance over the world's economic affairs. The guiding principle at that time was the belief that free trade promoted international prosperity and peace. Once the Cold War ended and communism in Europe had collapsed, globalization expanded as the former countries of the Soviet Bloc became integrated into Western European society. And China, the world's largest communist state, moved toward a market-based economy. All of this was bound up in a neoliberal policy in which free markets were paramount, and government's role was to reduce regulations on companies so that products and money could move more freely across borders. Expanding trade, the logic went, would expand wealth, and rising wealth would "trickle down" from the producers, business owners, and corporations to everyone else.

Text-Dependent Questions

1. When did the Berlin Wall come down?

2. What is Charter 77?

3. Who was Mikhail Gorbachev?

Research Projects

1. Research and create a list of five to ten books that influenced the feminist movement of the 1960s and 1970s. Create a table, including the titles, their authors, the dates of publication, and what the central themes were. Use several sources to ensure that you are gaining an objective analysis of the books.

2. Research and write a report about how the culture of other countries has been influenced by the United States. You can also focus just on your community.

WORDS TO UNDERSTAND

e-commerce: commercial transactions conducted over the Internet.

heretics: people who don't believe what is most commonly accepted.

interlopers: people who don't belong.

minarets: spires of mosques used for the summons to prayer in Islam.

puritanical: highly strict in a moral or religious sense.

relativism: belief in changeable standards.

universalism: belief in universal or global standards.

ABOVE: A Starbucks coffee shop—a symbol of globalization—can be found in the middle of the Forbidden City, one of the oldest districts in Beijing, China.

CHAPTER
5

Globalization and Today's Challenges

Globalizing forces, which helped to bring an end to the Cold War, were shaped by the speed with which people could communicate and disseminate information. The emergence of the World Wide Web in the early 1990s changed the way people, governments, and companies received and shared information.

Led by such companies as Apple and Microsoft, the digital revolution allowed businesses to expand and generate greater profits. The Internet made it easier for people to exchange currency, data, and ideas, the fundamental underpinnings of globalization. Post–Cold War globalization also made it much easier to travel from one end of the globe to the other. As a result, many left their home countries in search of better jobs, while others escaped oppressive regimes in their homelands. Yet globalization had become something more than an economic phenomenon. As borders blurred, the Internet, media, and the ease of international travel allowed people from different cultures to share music, art, language, religion, and literature.

The flip side of this utopia, however, was cultural imperialism, in which a powerful nation with economic might can easily spread its ideas and culture across borders. Many say that the United States has been in such a position since the 1990s, when globalization rapidly changed the shape of the world's economic and cultural landscape. Through the "free market" of ideas and products—enhanced through the Internet and other globalizing forces—the United States has been able to spread its products—be they electronic devices, music, or movies—across the globe.

Others argue that it's not as simple as that, however, and reality is much more nuanced. In fact, many cultures have been able to take global products and make them their own. This phenomenon, called glocalization, explains how local communities adapt a global product or service for their own specific culture. Glocalization allows global and local forces to converge. For example, McDonald's menus in India do not include beef or pork on the menu, which is important for religious reasons, and they also offer vegetarian dishes featuring curry sauces.

Globalizing Music

Music travels freely around the globe in the twenty-first century and adapts easily to local culture, producing many hybrid forms. Popular music during the 1960s spread across the Western world rapidly: as discussed above, the Beatles took their sound from Britain, to Germany and the United States, then around the world. The group also adopted influences from Asia, as George Harrison learned how to play the sitar from Indian musician Ravi Shankar.

By the early 2000s, this trend had magnified and intensified. "World music," a term popularized in the 1980s, had awakened interest in Asian, African, Arab, and Latin American music across the globe. The music of the Caribbean—salsa from Puerto Rico and Cuba, and ska and reggae from Jamaica—traveled north and east across the ocean to European dance floors. Appreciation for reggae, in fact, began earlier, in the mid-twentieth century, as waves of Jamaicans migrated to Britain after World War II. From there, it spread to Europe, North Africa, and the rest of Africa, where it was adapted to various forms of African music.

Global reggae star Bob Marley memorialized on postage stamp in the African country of Mozambique.

Hip-hop, itself having influences of Jamaican music, became one of the most vibrant transcultural art forms of the 2010s. Beginning in New York City, in the Bronx, with disenfranchised young black men, it was an underground form and, to some, deeply disturbing, as it narrated the harsh realities of ghetto life. It was adopted—some say co-opted—by big record companies in the United States, and by the 1990s it had become mainstream entertainment across the world.

One can even see echoes of it in "Gangnam Style," the song and music video by South Korean pop artist Psy, who satirizes the materialistic culture of the newly rich in the Gangnam district of Seoul, the country's capital. The music video, in 2012, was the first YouTube video to hit 1 billion views.

South Korean rapper Psy (far left) performs on the *Today Show* at Rockefeller Plaza in New York City in 2013.

A Digital Divide

People in wealthy societies take digital technology for granted. They can log on to the Internet and watch YouTube whenever they want—at home or at school, with a variety of different devices. They can talk on smartphones as they walk down the street or sit in a restaurant. They can conduct business with companies and people across the globe. This connectivity holds much promise in our current era—a promise, however, that sometimes fall short of expectations.

Digital technology has turned the world into a much smaller place. Not everyone, however, has the same access to technology, and a "digital divide" exists between poor and affluent nations. When people lack access to the Internet or digital devices, they can experience cultural, economic, and political barriers. The problems are worse in some countries than others. For example, according to Vanderbilt University, 36 percent of the Mexican population is connected to the Internet, and less than 17 percent of all Mexicans have online access at home. Although the gap between Mexicans who have Internet access and those who do not has narrowed in recent years, Mexico, Latin America's second-largest economy, lags far behind other Latin American nations, including Honduras, Guatemala, Brazil, Costa Rica, and others. Across the world, the United Nations says some 4 billion people—more than half the world's population—do not have Internet access.

Web access has become a critical part of social progress in developing countries. It helps them participate fully in the benefits of globalization. Business opportunities can often expand through the use of online marketing and **e-commerce**. Educational

Education without access to the Internet leaves students, such as these in Tanzania in 2015, unprepared for fully participating in contemporary life.

opportunities can increase as well, such as online college course offerings, called "massive open online courses." These MOOCs, as they are called, are popular among college students from across the world—from India and China to Kenya and Brazil. One of the most popular services is the nonprofit edX platform, which offers courses from many U.S.–based universities, such as Harvard, the Sorbonne in France, and Delft University of Technology in the Netherlands. Some experts, however, raise questions about relying on MOOCs and other online innovations as a solution for developing countries. They say that with such opportunities available online, many countries will not develop their own educational systems.

Protecting Cultural Heritage and Indigenous Groups

The world is full of cultural sites, some that date back to the dawn of humanity itself. In recent years, however, many of these sites have become endangered for one reason or another, usually by human activities. Recent turmoil in the Middle East, for example, has not only dislodged people from their homes and destroyed families, it has also caused the destruction of ancient archaeological sites.

In 2015, the so-called Islamic State (ISIS), a terrorist group, destroyed the Temple of Baalshamin, in Palmyra, one of the major cultural centers in Syria. ISIS terrorists also damaged another temple and Iraq's Mosul Museum, which housed stone statues that dated from about 100 BCE to 100 CE. The group claimed it destroyed these and other historic sites because they were symbols of idol worship, which is against their version of Islam.

Whether it is the Middle East, South America, North America, or Asia, some things are so important that they need international protection. Some have economic as well as cultural value. Others impact humans emotionally because they are part of our shared human tradition and culture. Some are buildings. Some are songs. Others are pieces of art. The United Nations Educational, Scientific and Cultural Organization (UNESCO) has taken a lead role in protecting these cultural treasures. The United Nations formed UNESCO in 1945 because it felt the world's culture needed to be saved in an often violent world. While its initial job was to rebuild schools, libraries, and museums after the devastation caused by World War II, UNESCO in 1972 sponsored an international agreement to establish a list—the World Heritage List—of cultural and natural sites that needed protecting. Every continent has varied sites that are included on the list, such as the Belize Barrier Reef and the Acropolis of Athens in Greece.

Some of what UNESCO tries to protect falls into the category of "intangible cultural heritage," such as the Sbek Thom, a Cambodian shadow theater that features leather puppets; the Baltic Song and Dance Celebrations in Latvia, Estonia, and Lithuania, which highlight performing folk art; and barkcloth making in Uganda, which involves a prehistoric weaving technique.

The UN has also had a hand in increasing awareness of the rights of indigenous groups, recognizing that the very survival of some of these peoples depend on protecting livelihoods and cultural practices. The United Nations solidified its approach to these concerns when the UN Declaration on the Rights of Indigenous Peoples was adopted in 2007. Despite this increased recognition by the UN and on the global stage, exploitation persists.

SMILE—YOU'RE ON YOUTUBE

Founded in 2005, the video-sharing site YouTube has had an enormous impact on the world's culture. People can record videos on their laptops or cell phones and upload them to the site. Often the videos spread within hours to every corner of the world. YouTube also allows people to share music videos, television shows, recorded book reviews, movies, and other forms of entertainment. The service has become so pervasive and popular that many have become so-called YouTube celebrities. For example, a British girl named Zoe Sugg, also known as Zoella, had 270 million views in 2014 as she sat on her bed and offered viewers beauty and shopping tips.

While many of the videos are just silly, others can be informative. Videos taken by protesters during the Arab Spring rebellions in the Middle East and North Africa in 2011 helped them to organize and galvanize world opinion against the region's oppressive governments in a matter of days. Many videos also find their way into public media as news stories, advertisements, and entertainment shows. In 2015, YouTube had more than a billion users, with 80 percent of all views coming from outside the United States.

The Temple of Baalshamin, in Palmyra, one of the most important cultural centers in Syria, was destroyed by ISIS in 2015.

In Brazil, for example, a vast dam project called Belo Monte, approved in 2011, will eventually divert 80 percent of the Xingu River in efforts to increase hydroelectric power in the country. By the time it is completed in 2019, however, it will destroy 932 square miles (2,414 square kilometers) of rainforest, according to Amazon Watch, and force 20,000 to 40,000 indigenous people from their ancestral homes.

Religious Friction

Friction between different religions and cultures has been on the rise in recent years as people of various backgrounds migrate due to economic or personal security issues. While there has always been tension when religions and cultures mingle, globalization has exacerbated the problem.

The migration of Muslims to non-Muslim countries is one example. The conflicts associated with this transcultural mixing can be traced to the roots of political Islam. During the Cold War, the West and the Soviet Union eyed the Muslim world not only for its oil, but also as a strategic region in a geopolitical puzzle. Many Muslims living in those countries viewed the superpowers with suspicion and reacted militantly through political organizing, often in opposition to the Arab governments in power. Globalization, which spread Western ideas and values throughout Islamic countries, was also an irritant that helped increase radicalization of Muslim militancy.

The rise of political Islam continued unabated for more than forty years, and in some cases became extreme. Radical Islamic groups, such as al-Qaeda, began forcefully and violently pushing their cultural and political agendas under an extreme version of Islamic law called Sharia. As a result, Muslim extremists have targeted other religious groups for persecution, including Christians, as well as sects of Islam that they don't agree with. ISIS, for example, has murdered and displaced the Yazidis, Mandaeans, and other small religious groups in Iraq and Syria.

By the same token, Muslims coming to Europe and the United States have also been persecuted. In the view of many Westerners, people of different faiths are **interlopers** who threaten the stability and order of society. Assimilation has been difficult. Muslims, for example, have been looked on with suspicion since the September 11, 2001, terrorist attacks in New York City and Washington, D.C.

Moreover, Europe's ever-expanding Muslim population, rapidly increasing due to unrest in Africa and the Middle East, has spurred debate on a variety of issues ranging from immigration to assimilation and cultural identity. Terrorist attacks in Europe and elsewhere have fueled anti-Muslim backlashes and deepened tensions. One result has been that some politicians, such as those in France and Switzerland, among other nations, have called for a ban on the construction of **minarets** and mosques, and on the wearing of veils or headscarves, as the French did in 2010.

Although European countries have partially succeeded in integrating new groups like Muslim guest workers and their families, many young Muslims who traveled to Europe from North Africa or the Middle East are alienated from the mainstream European culture and society around them. This has provided terrorist organizations, such as ISIS, with a pool of new recruits, which they aggressively enlist through online propaganda and personal persuasion. Many Muslim terrorists in Europe, indeed, are homegrown.

Cultural Relativism versus Universal Rights

The debate between so-called cultural **universalism** and cultural **relativism** is one of the chief challenges of the twenty-first century. Are human rights universal? Do all societies and cultures share the same idea about what human rights are? Should they? Or are human rights culturally dependent? Does each society have to abide by the same moral principles, or can they be different?

Newly commissioned lieutenants in the Afghan Air Force in 2010, these women are all wearing a hijab, a kind of veil typical of Muslim women. Some people in Western societies are uncomfortable with such outward signs of religious devotion.

THE EXTREMISM OF WAHHABISM

One of the most conservative—some would say *puritanical*—forms of Islam is Wahhabism, which for more than two hundred years has been the dominant faith of Saudi Arabia. Named after Muhammad ibn 'Abd al-Wahhab, an eighteenth-century Islamic preacher, Wahhabism demands that its followers adhere strictly to a literal interpretation of the Koran, the Muslim holy book. Many terrorists—including Osama bin Laden, the mastermind of the 9/11 attacks—are Wahhabists, who believe that those who do not practice their form of religion are *heretics*. They believe in a "pure Islam" that does not deviate from Sharia law. Many Muslims, however, believe that such fundamentalism has distorted Islam's true meaning.

Pope Francis I, the leader of the Roman Catholic Church, warned against the "tyranny of relativism" in 2013. He said, "There cannot be true peace if everyone . . . can always claim exclusively his own rights, without at the same time caring for the good of others, of everyone, on the basis of the nature that unites every human being on this earth."

In 1948 the United Nations, through the Universal Declaration of Human Rights, established a set of principles that tried to answer these questions. It articulates the same rights for all people, regardless of who they are or where they live.

Others, however, have weighed in with a different version of humans rights. They say that the West's version—enshrined in the UN Declaration—focuses too much on individual rights and not on what is good for society as a whole. China, which values social cohesion, for instance, questions the importance the West places on individual expression above all else. In fact, some say that human rights should be determined by each country, taking cultural values into account. Many argue that universalism is a form of cultural imperialism, as some nations, specifically in the West, try to extend their cultural beliefs over other peoples and societies. Many Muslims in France make this argument in reference to the controversy, mentioned above, surrounding the use of veils by women in public. France, as a nation, values openness and individuality, but a veil worn in public is a sign of modesty for Islamic women—a trait valued by Muslims worldwide. How is one group's value worth more than another's?

These issues become more and more relevant as globalization brings more people, from different cultures, faiths, and continents, into contact with each other. Through migration, travel, online connections, and business dealings, we are more connected than ever before. Dealing with this cultural dissonance is critical to taking full advantage of globalization and to living peacefully in the twenty-first century.

Text-Dependent Questions

1. Describe the job of UNESCO.

2. Name two ways that digital technology can help a society.

3. What is glocalization?

Research Projects

1. Create a computer slide show illustrating how the Internet and digital technology has affected your life, your family, and your school.

2. Research UNESCO's World Heritage list (http://whc.unesco.org/en/list/) and explore one of the places on it. Write a report describing what is culturally important about the site, how it is in danger, and what is being done to save it.

Timeline

1944	The first media reports brings to the world's attention the horrors of the Holocaust, when the Soviet Army begins liberating Nazi death camps in Eastern Europe.
1945	An American B-29 bomber named the Enola Gay drops the world's first atomic bomb on the Japanese city of Hiroshima.
1948	The UN adopts the Universal Declaration of Human Rights (UDHR) and aims to ensure the concept of universal humanity.
1950	The Congress for Cultural Freedom is established in the United States, one year after the Cultural and Scientific Conference for World Peace in New York City causes a stir.
1950s	The "Beats," a group of writers and thinkers, rail against the blandness of middle-class life, criticizing suburbia, and materialism.
	After consumerism takes hold in the United States, Japan and Western Europe follow suit, spurred by reconstruction and redevelopment of their economic systems.
	West Germany's "economic miracle," or Wirtschaftswunder, leads Germans living in communist East Germany to flee for the West through Berlin.
mid-1950s	A new, more promising era in the Soviet Union begins, thanks to a thaw under Nikita Khrushchev, who relaxes the government's repression of artistic and cultural expression.
1957	There are about 40 million television sets in the United States, compared to 8,000 eleven years earlier.
1959	*Hiroshima Mon Amour* (*Hiroshima My Love*), directed by French filmmaker Alain Resnais, is released; it deals with antiwar themes following the dropping of the atomic bombs on Japan.
	The Kitchen Debate takes place between U.S. vice president Richard Nixon and Soviet premier Nikita Khrushchev.
1960	By the end of this year—Africa's "Year of Freedom"—there are twenty-seven African countries that had gained independence from colonial powers.
1961	Cosmonaut Yuri Gagarin returns to Earth, after becoming the first human in space; his welcome home celebration is widely televised, in the Soviet Union and other countries as well.
	Frantz Fanon publishes *The Wretched of the Earth*, an analysis of how colonization impacted the psychological health of individuals.
	The Beatles begin to gain attention Hamburg, Germany, in 1961, and to develop a unique musical style.

1963	*The Feminine Mystique* by Betty Friedan is published; it is one of the first books to explore women's lives and identities.
1964	The Group of 77 forms at the UN to help the developing world gain more power on the world stage.
1965	The UN establishes the UN Development Programme, which begins to take cultural and social factors into account when analyzing development and well-being.
mid-1960s	The Beatles make a connection to the Maharishi Mahesh Yogi, who has developed a form of spirituality called Transcendental Meditation.
1966	A literary journal called *Souffles* is founded by Moroccan poet Abdellatif Laâbi; it allows its contributors to diverge from the traditional literary world.
	The UN General Assembly adopts the International Covenant on Civil and Political Rights (ICCPR) and the International Covenant on Economic, Social and Cultural Rights (ICESCR).
1968	Activists clash with police and National Guard outside the Democratic National Convention in Chicago, as they protest the Vietnam War.
	French student protesters take over several universities to protest the educational system, capitalism, and joblessness; the protests spread to France's industrial centers and factories, effectively shutting down the national economy.
1969	The Woodstock Music and Art Fair takes place on Max Yasgur's farm in upstate New York; it is billed as three days of peace, love, and rock 'n' roll.
1970s	The widening use of the birth control pill means that women can have sex without worrying about getting pregnant.
1971	Relations between China—the world's most populous communist nation—and the United States begins to thaw when the U.S. ping-pong team visits China.
1972	The United Nations Educational, Scientific and Cultural Organization (UNESCO) establishes the World Heritage List, include cultural that needed protecting.
1989	The Berlin Wall, separating communist East Berlin from the West and long a symbol of Cold War tensions, is torn down; two years later, the Soviet Union collapses.
1990s	"World music" has awakened interest in Asian, African, Arab, and Latin American music across the globe.
2007	The United Nations passes the UN Declaration on the Rights of Indigenous Peoples.
2012	"Gangnam Style," the song and music video by South Korean pop artist Psy, satirizes the materialistic culture of the rich elite in Seoul, the country's capital; the music video is the first YouTube video to hit 1 billion views.
2015	The terrorist group Islamic State (ISIS) destroys the Temple of Baalshamin, in Palmyra, one of the major cultural centers in Syria during the Syrian civil war.

Further Research

BOOKS

Ervan, Justin, and Zachary A. Smith. *Globalization: A Reference Handbook*. Santa Barbara, CA: ABC-CLIO, 2008.

Pekar, Harvey, and Paul Buhle. *The Beats: A Graphic History*. New York: Hill and Wang, 2009.

Poiger, Uta G. *Jazz, Rock, and Rebels: Cold War Politics and American Culture in a Divided Germany*. Berkeley: University of California Press., 2000.

Swingrover, E. A. *The Counterculture Reader*. London: Pearson/Longman, 2003.

ONLINE

International Work Group for Indigenous Affairs: "Who Are the Indigenous Peoples?": http://www.iwgia.org/culture-and-identity/identification-of-indigenous-peoples.

Poetry Foundation: "Allen Ginsburg, 1926–1997": http://www.poetryfoundation.org/bio/allen-ginsberg.

Rolling Stone: "Bob Dylan, the Beatles, and the Rock of the Sixties": http://www.rollingstone.com/music/news/bob-dylan-the-beatles-and-the-rock-roll-of-the-60s-19900823.

UNESCO World Heritage List: http://whc.unesco.org/en/list/.

"Who Are Indigenous Peoples?": http://www.firstpeoples.org/who-are-indigenous-peoples/the-indigenous-movement.

NOTE TO EDUCATORS: This book contains both imperial and metric measurements as well as references to global practices and trends in an effort to encourage the student to gain a worldly perspective. We, as publishers, feel it's our role to give young adults the tools they need to thrive in a global society.

Index

Italicized page numbers refer to illustrations

A

Africa 26–28, 33, 43
African Americans 24, 31, 33
Americans for Intellectual Freedom 20, *20*
Amnesty International 42, *43*
Arnaz, Desi 24, *24*
artists and writers 11, 19–21, 23, 26–28, 31–32, 43, 49
Asia 12, 14–15, 26, 33, 50. *See also* China
atomic age *10,* 10–11, 19, 45

B

Ball, Lucille 24, *24*
Beat Generation 33–34, *34*
Beatles *36,* 36–38, 50
Beatniks 31
Brando, Marlon *33,* 33–34
Britain 26, 35, 45
Brown, Helen Gurley 42

C

capitalism 19, 23, 35
Charter 77 declaration 43, *44*
China 9, 28, 45–46, *48,* 56
Civil Rights Movement (U.S.) 31, 34–35
Cold War 10, 19–28, 32–34, 45–46, 49
colonialism 26–28
communism 10, 19–21, 23, 25, 32–33, 35
conformity 23, 31, 33–34
consumerism 21–23, *22,* 31
counterculture (1960s) 31–37
cultural artifacts and heritage 10, 18, *18,* 52–53, *54*
cultural imperialism 49, 56
cultural norms and values 10, 27
cultural relativism 55–56
Czechoslovakia and Czech Republic 38, *38,* 43, *44*

D

de Beauvoir, Simone 42
Democratic National Convention (Chicago, 1968) 38
Dietrich, Marlene 13, *14*
digital technology 49, 51–52, *52*
Dub ek, Alexander 38

E

education 28, 51–52, *52*
environmentalism 35
Europe 9–10, 14–15, 20–23, 25–27, 32, 34–35, 46, 55

F

Fanon, Frantz 27, *28*
Female Eunuch, The (Greer) 41, *42*
Feminine Mystique, The (Friedan) 41
film and filmmakers *10,* 10–11, 31–34, *33*
France 11, 15, 35–37, *36,* 55–56
Francis I (pope) *56*
Friedan, Betty 41

G

Gagarin, Yuri 25, *25*
gay rights 35, 41–45
Germany 9, 14–16, 22, 26, 35–38, 45, *46,* 50
Ginsberg, Allen 33, 35, *35*
globalization *48,* 49–56
glocalization 49
Gorbachev, Mikhail 31–32, 45–46
Great Depression 19, 21, 31
Greer, Germaine 41, *42*
Gulag Archipelago, The (Solzhenitsyn) 32

H

Harrer, Heinrich 12–13
Harrison, George 36–37, 50
Havel, Václav 43, *44*
human rights 15–16, 41–45, 53, 56
Human Rights Watch 42

I

I Love Lucy 24, *24*
immigration 54–55
India 28, 37–38
indigenous peoples 41, 52–53
Internet 49, 51–52, *52*
Islam 27, 55–56. *See also* Muslims
Islamic State (ISIS) 52, *54,* 55

J

Japan 9–11, 22
Japanese-Americans *12*

K

Kerouac, Jack 33
Khrushchev, Nikita 23, *23,* 31–32
Kitchen Debate *23,* 23–24
Kommune 1 (West Germany) 35–37
Krautrock movement 36

Index (continued)

Laâbi, Abdellatif 27, *27*
Lenin, Vladimir 26
Lennon, John 36

M

Maharishi Mahesh Yogi 37, *38*
Mailer, Norman 20
Man in the Gray Flannel Suit (Wilson) 31
Mao Zedong 28, 35, 45
Marley, Bob *50*
McCartney, Paul 36
media 13–15, *15, 18,* 24–26, 37–38, 42
Middle East 26, 45, 52–53
Miller, Arthur 20
Morocco 27
music 11, 13–15, *14, 30,* 31, 34, 36–38, 49–50, *50–51*
Muslims 27, 54–56

N

nationalist movements 26–27, 33
Native Americans 33, 41–45
Nazi Germany 9, 14. *See also* Germany
New Left politics 35, 38
new world order 10, 46
1984 (Orwell) 26
Nixon, Richard 23, *23,* 45
nuclear weapons 10, 19, 35, 45

O

One Day in the Life of Ivan Denisovich (Solzhenitsyn) 32, *32*
Organization of Arab Petroleum Exporting Countries (OAPEC) 45
Orwell, George 26

P

political activism 34–35, *36,* 37
propaganda 13, 19–21, 25, 55

R

race and racism 26–27
religion 14, 27, 49, 54–56, *55, 56*
reproductive rights 41–42
Richmond, Yale 21

S

Salinger, J. D. 23
Saunders, Frances Stonor 19–20
science fiction *10,* 11
Second Sex, The (de Beauvoir) 42

September 11, 2001 terrorist attacks 55–56
Seven Years in Tibet (Harrer) 12–13
Shankar, Ravi 37, 50
Solzhenitsyn, Aleksandr 32, *32*
Souffles (Morocco) 27
Soviet Union 9, 14, 20–21, *21,* 26–27, 31–32, 38, *38,* 43–46
Stalin, Joseph 20–21, 26, 32
Starr, Ringo 36
Students for a Democratic Society 35
Suri, Jeremi 34

T

television and radio 13, *15, 18,* 24–25, *24–25,* 32

U

underground press 36–37
United Nations 15–16, *16,* 43, 53, 56
United States 11, *12,* 19–22, 27, 32–33, 38, 45–46, 49
universal rights 55–56

V

Vietnam War 35, 38, 45

W

Wahhabism 56
Warhol, Andy 23
Wilson, Sloan 31
women 28, 31, 35, *40,* 41–45
Woodstock Music and Art Fair (1969) 37
World War II *8,* 9–15, *14, 15,* 31, 53
Wretched of the Earth, The (Fanon) 27

Y

YouTube 51, 53

Photo Credits

Page number	Page location	Archive/Photographer
8	Top	Wikimedia Commons/U.S. Army
10	Bottom	Wikimedia Commons/Toho Company Ltd.
12	Top	Wikimedia Commons/442nd RCT Archives
13	Bottom	Wikimedia Commons/Smokeonthewater
14	Top	Wikimedia Commons/George Grantham Bain Collection (Library of Congress)
15	Top	Library of Congress/Esther Bubley
16	Bottom	Wikimedia Commons/Yann
18	Top	Wikimedia Commons/Motorola
20	Bottom	Wikimedia Commons/Roger & Renate Rössing
21	Top	Wikimedia Commons/Alexander Makarov
22	Top	iStock/Lisa-Blue
23	Bottom	National Archives and Records Administration/Richard Nixon Library
24	Bottom	Wikimedia Commons/Macfadden Publications
25	Top	Wikimedia Commons/Leszek Wysznacki
27	Bottom	Wikimedia Commons/Ji-Elle
28	Top	Wikimedia Commons
30	Top	Library of Congress, Prints & Photographs Division, New York World-Telegram and the Sun Newspaper Collection
32	Bottom	Wikimedia Commons/Dutch National Archives, Bert Berhoeff
33	Top	Wikimedia Commons/Midnight bird
34	Bottom	Wikimedia Commons/William P. Gottlieb (Library of Congress)
35	Top	Wikimedia Commons/Dutch National Archives, Hans van Dijk
36	Top	Wikimedia Commons/GeorgeLouis
36	Bottom	Wikimedia Commons/Jennifer Boyer
38	Top	Wikimedia Commons/Keithbob
38	Bottom	Wikimedia Commons/Szilas
40	Top	Library of Congress/Warren K. Leffler
42	Top	Wikimedia Commons/Dutch National Archives, Hans Peters
43	Top	Shutterstock/paintings
44	Full page	Wikimedia Commons/David Sedlecký
46	Top	Wikimedia Commons/Raphaël Thiémard
48	Top	Wikimedia Commons/Mr. Tickle
50	Top	Shutterstock/Olga Popova
51	Top	Shutterstock/Debby Wong
52	Top	Shutterstock/Dietmar Temps
54	Top	Wikimedia Commons/Vernard Gagnon
55	Bottom	Wikimedia Commons/Mass Communications Specialist First Class Elizabeth Burke (U.S. Armed Forces)
56	Bottom	Wikimedia Commons/Alfredo Borba
Cover	Top	Wikimedia Commons
Cover	Left	Wikimedia Commons/Mark Taylor
Cover	Right	Shutterstock/Crystal Home

About the Author and Advisor

Series Advisor

Ruud van Dijk teaches the history of international relations at the University of Amsterdam, the Netherlands. He studied history at Amsterdam, the University of Kansas, and Ohio University, where he obtained his Ph.D. in 1999. He has also taught at Carnegie Mellon University, Dickinson College, and the University of Wisconsin-Milwaukee, where he also served as editor at the Center for 21st Century Studies. He has published on the East-West conflict over Germany during the Cold War, the controversies over nuclear weapons in the 1970s and 1980s, and on the history of globalization. He is the senior editor of the *Encyclopedia of the Cold War* (2008), produced with MTM Publishing and published by Routledge.

Author

John Perritano is an award-winning journalist, writer, and editor from Southbury, Connecticut, who has written numerous articles and books on a variety of subjects, including history, politics, and culture, for such publishers as Mason Crest, National Geographic, Scholastic, and *Time/Life*. His articles have appeared on Discovery.com, PopularMechanics.com, and other magazines and websites. He holds a master's degree in American History from Western Connecticut State University.